S0-BJP-234

Cutting and Self-Mutilation

Other titles in the Teen Issues *series:*

Addiction
The "High" That Brings You Down
ISBN 0-89490-915-0

AIDS & HIV
Risky Business
ISBN 0-89490-917-7

Brothers and Sisters
Born to Bicker?
ISBN 0-89490-914-2

Conflict Resolution
The Win-Win Situation
ISBN 0-7660-1584-X

Cybersafety
Surfing Safely Online
ISBN 0-7660-1580-7

Depression
What It Is, How to Beat It
ISBN 0-7660-1357-X

Difficult People
Dealing With Almost Anyone
ISBN 0-7660-1583-1

Eating Disorders and Weight Control
ISBN 0-89490-919-3

Focus on Body Image
How You Feel About How You Look
ISBN 0-7660-1915-2

Friends, Cliques, and Peer Pressure
Be True to Yourself
ISBN 0-7660-1669-2

Money
Save It, Manage It, Spend It
ISBN 0-7660-1363-4

Racism and Ethnic Bias
Everybody's Problem
ISBN 0-7660-1578-5

Romantic Breakup
It's Not the End of the World
ISBN 0-7660-1361-8

The Rules to Be Cool
Etiquette and Netiquette
ISBN 0-7660-1607-2

School Violence
Deadly Lessons
ISBN 0-7660-1358-8

Sexual Abuse and Incest
ISBN 0-89490-916-9

Stepfamilies
How a New Family Works
ISBN 0-7660-1666-8

Stress
Just Chill Out!
ISBN 0-89490-918-5

SuicideWise
Taking Steps Against Teen Suicide
ISBN 0-7660-1360-X

Tattooing and Body Piercing
Understanding the Risks
ISBN 0-7660-1668-4

Teen Consumer Smarts
Shop, Save, and Steer Clear of Scams
ISBN 0-7660-1667-6

Teens With Single Parents
Why Me?
ISBN 0-89490-913-4

Cutting and Self-Mutilation

When Teens Injure Themselves

Kathleen Winkler

Enslow Publishers, Inc.
40 Industrial Road
Box 398
Berkeley Heights, NJ 07922
USA

PO Box 38
Aldershot
Hants GU12 6BP
UK

http://www.enslow.com

Library of Congress Cataloging-in-Publication Data

Winkler, Kathleen.
Cutting and self-mutilation : when teens injure themselves / Kathleen Winkler.
p. cm.—(Teen issues)
Includes bibliographical references and index.
Contents: Parker's story—What is this thing called self-injury?—Why do people do this?—Mental illness linked with self-injury—Dangers in self-injury—Treating people who self-injure—When a friend self-injures.
ISBN-10: 0-7660-1956-X
1. Self-mutilation—Juvenile literature. [1. Self-mutilation.] I. Title. II. Series.
RJ506.S44 W56 2002
616.85'82—dc21

2002002918

ISBN-13: 978-0-7660-1956-0

Printed in the United States of America

10 9 8 7 6 5

To Our Readers:
We have done our best to make sure all Internet Addresses in this book were active and appropriate when we went to press. However, the author and the publisher have no control over and assume no liability for the material available on those Internet sites or on other Web sites they may link to. Any comments or suggestions can be sent by e-mail to comments@enslow.com or to the address on the back cover.

Illustration Credits: Corel Corporation, pp. 17, 18, 25; Courtesy of Dr. George Korkos, p. 35; Eyewire, p. 8; Enslow Publishers, Inc., p. 31; Ralph and Kathleen Winkler, pp. 41, 43, 49, 52.

Cover Photo: Skjold Photos.

Contents

1

Parker's Story

Parker sits in a chair in her therapist's office. She is a slender, long-haired young woman in a simple denim skirt. Her makeup-free face looks far younger than her actual age, in her mid-twenties. She looks out the window watching cars and people coming and going from the busy office building. The therapist's office with its plump couch and soft sand-beige color scheme is an island of quiet and calm in a busy world.

Parker's gray-blue eyes take on a distant gaze as she thinks back over the long path she has followed since the day she first stepped through the doors of a bustling junior high school. Inside those doors she did not find calm. Nor did she find the support and friendship she hoped for. Instead she stood alone, as if in a glass bubble, while the life of the school whirled about her. She pounded the walls of the bubble, crying inside: "Would somebody please notice me? Would somebody please be my friend?"

Starting a new school can be overwhelming for anyone, but when a teen does not know anybody it can be even harder and more stressful.

Finally, Parker found a way to express her hurt and isolation. But it was not a very healthy way. It was a way that hurt her even more. She cut her arms.

"I grew up in a typical family—there were two kids and a dog. My parents are still married today; I had both my grandparents and lots of other family," she says. "We kind of got along, at least we kept peace in the house."

Parker was happy in elementary school. She knew everybody and was comfortable there. But after sixth-grade graduation, it was time to start a new adventure that fall: junior high.

"Suddenly I knew almost nobody and it was very stressful," she says. "I was shy to begin with, always quiet, and all those new people seemed to know each other already. I didn't know what to do. I went from class to class and did my work and that was about it."

Looking back, Parker thinks she could have coped with the strain of a new school if she had more family support. But her family, she says, did not relate to each other very well. Her parents both did their own thing. Her father spent most of his time in his basement workroom while her mother sulked because he was not paying attention to her.

"I didn't know how to relate to other people because I didn't have a very good role model at home," Parker says. "I tried playing soccer. I didn't know the girls and I didn't feel comfortable around them. I didn't like being there. So I quit. That's when I started feeling kind of depressed. I started to have a fascination with kind of depressing stuff—I drew pictures of ways to kill myself, things like that. I would stay focused on that when I had nobody to talk to."

It was not long before her obsession with morbid things turned to action. "It was about halfway through seventh grade," she remembers. "I read a story about somebody who committed suicide by slashing their wrists, so I did that. I didn't really want to die so I came out with barely a scratch."

But that, she says, was her introduction to hurting herself. "I used a scissors that first time. But it didn't help because I just felt disgusted with myself," she says. "I thought, 'You are pathetic. You don't have the guts to really do anything.' It took a while, but then I did it again. And that time it started to make me feel better." People who cut themselves often say it makes them feel better, but as we will see, it is not a real solution for problems and, in the end, makes them worse.

By ninth grade, Parker was cutting herself more regularly. As she went through high school, she cut herself more and more often, until she was doing it at least every other week.

"Nobody ever noticed the cuts," she says. "I would always wear long sleeves. Once I was in a performing group and we had to wear sleeveless dresses. I was very careful about how I carried my arms and nobody said anything about the scars."

But one night Parker decided to try something more drastic. She heated up her curling iron and held it against her arm. "That's how I got caught, because that burn showed," she says. "A friend of mine, Sherry, saw the burn and asked me about it. I told her I'd gotten the curling iron tangled up and dropped it on my arm, but I guess she didn't believe me. She said something to her parents and they said something to my parents. Then it got ugly."

Parker's mother confronted her. "She said to me, 'Sherry said you burned your arm.' My stomach dropped but I just kept watching TV like it was no big deal. Before I knew it she was yelling at me that she wanted to see it. My father just kept reading the newspaper. My brother kind of held me down so they could see my arm."

The next day when Parker got home from school, her mother told her they were going to see a therapist. But Parker would never talk to the therapist about what she had done and why. The "therapy" soon ended.

After graduation, Parker headed off to college. During her four years, she managed to do her work, get good grades, even make a few friends. But all the while she continued to secretly cut herself. She chose to live in a single room in her dorm so she could shut out the rest of the world while she did her cutting.

"At that point I had pretty much accepted that this is who I am and I don't know any other way to be," she remembers. "But toward the end of college I was lucky enough to work as a research assistant for a psychology professor who was an expert in depression." He must have picked up on Parker's stress and unhappiness. As they became friends, he started asking her questions about how she slept and how she ate, and what was the longest time she had ever been happy. "It was the first real help I ever had. I was with him for about eight months and he helped me work through a lot of stuff, especially about my parents. It seemed to work pretty well for a while—I was healthy and feeling good for the first time in my life."

Parker's "break" from hurting herself lasted three years. She graduated and got a teaching job. "And then it all came back," she says. "I had a pretty stressful work situation. It was hard to go to work every day. I just couldn't handle it. I went to a regular doctor and he prescribed a new antidepressant drug called Prozac but it didn't really help. Then I found a psychologist who knew what she was doing. The first real key for me was when she told me that I was not crazy. She said, 'You are sick and there's a way to help you and you can also help yourself.' Actually being able to talk about stuff to her, being with someone who knew the right questions to ask was what I needed." The psychologist also put her in touch with a psychiatrist to prescribe medication.

Parker has now been in therapy for four years. "The more I learn about this, the more I understand why I did some of that stuff," she says. "I feel like I'm past the big hump, but there are still a few issues I need to address. I'm going to be careful this time not to leave therapy too early because that's what I did in the past. The psychiatrist is giving me a different medication than the other doctor did. She is monitoring me closely and changed my dose until we found the right one. The biggest key is being with people who know what they are doing."

Parker is now married to a man who knows her history and is supportive. She has been injury-free for several years. Looking back, she finds it hard to believe some of the things she did. "You develop a pattern, a way of doing it," she recalls. "At first it was haphazard, when I'd start to get frustrated. But then you begin to realize what works for you. If you do it fast enough you don't really feel it. You just kind of close your eyes and grit your teeth. Later you get this sting, and it's actually a relief, comforting, because you aren't thinking about the reason you did it anymore. You're just feeling what happened. That's better than thinking about why you did it.

"Now, if I'm feeling anxious, I know what soothes me. I put on my headphones and listen to music and that calms me. I turn out the lights and just focus on the music because that's something I really like. I can also talk to my husband. It's good to have someone to lean on, to say, 'I'm having a rough day, I need to talk about it' and have somebody who knows and will listen."

Parker is happy to be free of the cutting that ruled her life for so long. But she knows that most people have a hard time understanding why people would deliberately harm their own bodies. She understands that most people are revolted by such an act. She wants that attitude to change.

"It's not a horrible thing," she says. "These people aren't monsters."

People who do this are not "crazy," she points out. It is a way of coping, of getting through life, although not a healthy one.[1]

In this book we will look at the issue of self-injury: why people do this to themselves and what can be done to help them.

2

What Is This Thing Called Self-Injury?

I started with banging my head against the wall; I started that in fourth grade. I would use door frames and window frames. Once I banged a coffee mug against my forehead. I started cutting when I was older. I had lost my job and one night I sat down on the couch and started slicing up my arm with a jackknife. I was feeling guilty about so many things. About losing my job and disappointing and abandoning my parents, and just being slime. I felt [by cutting] I was punishing myself and it was right that I should punish myself. Before I cut I always felt tense, anxious, nervous, barely able to think. Like I was wrapped with a million coats and lid on my head. I couldn't breathe. I remember once I took a silver cross and heated it in a flame and put it on my skin. It just went on for years and years even while I was getting help.

Diane, age 24, active self-injurer[1]

Diane is an example of a self-injurer. Other names for this behavior include self-inflicted violence or self-harm. It used to be called self-mutilation, but that term is not used much anymore. People who do this do not like that term because it implies that they want to permanently harm their bodies, and that is usually not true.[2]

Defining Self-Injury

Self-injury is defined as deliberately doing harm to one's own body, doing it alone (without the help of another person), and doing something serious enough to damage tissue and, often, leave a scar.[3]

Armando Favazza was a professor of psychiatry at the University of Missouri who did the earliest research on self-injury during the 1980s. He says there are three types of self-injury: episodic (happening only once in a while), repetitive (doing it often and thinking about it when not doing it), and compulsive (the person is not able to control it and may need medication to stop doing it).[4] Self-injury is usually classified as a repetitive behavior.

What Kinds of Things Do Self-Injurers Do?

There are many forms of self-injury, but the most common are cutting, burning, hitting, breaking bones, picking old wounds, and biting. Some mental health experts, including Dr. Favazza, also include pulling hair as a self-injury behavior; other experts do not. Dr. Favazza, along with colleague Karen Conterio, did a survey of what self-injurers actually do. This is what they found (the totals add up to more than 100 percent because most self-injurers do more than one thing):

- Cutting: 72 percent
- Burning: 35 percent
- Self-hitting: 30 percent
- Picking wounds: 22 percent
- Pulling hair: 10 percent
- Breaking bones: 8 percent[5]

What Kinds of People Self-Injure?

Most people respond to the thought of self-injury with revulsion and disbelief. They think the person who does such a thing must be "crazy." The word crazy, mental health professionals say, is not a medical term. It is a slang word that is usually meant to put someone down. Still, people often think that someone who self-injures is surely not the kind of person they would have as a friend or family member.

In a 2000 television movie about self-injury called *Secret Cutting*, one of the first to deal with this issue, students found out that Dawn, one of their classmates, cut herself. One student's response, was, "OOOOOOhh—freaky!!" Another girl chimed in, "That is SO beyond weird."[6] While the movie was fiction, the students' response was what self-injurers often have to deal with.

However, experts say that people who self-injure can seem very normal to the outside world. Their parents, families, and best friends often do not know what they are doing. Research shows that people who self-injure are often people who:

- dislike themselves
- become very upset by rejection

- are always angry, often at themselves, and hide it
- have aggressive feelings that they also hide
- are impulsive
- do not plan for the future very well
- are often depressed
- are often anxious
- are often irritable
- do not have very good skills for coping with stress
- do not think they have much control over their lives
- do not think of themselves as having much power[7]

While a person who has some of these symptoms is not necessarily a self-injurer, someone who has many of them should be evaluated by a mental health professional.

How Common Is Self-Injury?

"Because of the shame and secrecy surrounding this behavior, no one really knows how many people are self-mutilators," says Marilee Strong, author of a book on self-injury called *A Bright Red Scream: Self-Mutilation and the Language of Pain*. "But a conservative estimate is that at least two million Americans are chronically and repeatedly injuring themselves every year. That's thirty times the rate of suicide attempts and 140 times the rate of actual suicides."[8]

Estimates are higher in the teen population. Studies show that as many as 1,400 of every 100,000 people aged fifteen to thirty-five in the United States self-injure each year—that is over 2 million people. Dr. Favazza did a survey of 500 college students and found that 12 percent of them had hurt themselves at least once.[9]

People who self-injure are often depressed.

In people with some form of psychiatric illness the rate is much higher, up to 20 percent of all patients, and 40 to 61 percent of teenagers who are hospitalized for psychiatric problems. When therapists who work with patients in their offices (rather than hospitalized patients) were asked if they had ever seen someone who self-injured, almost half said yes.[10]

While men and boys do self-injure, the majority of self-injurers are women and girls. In Dr. Favazza's survey of 250 self-injurers, 96 percent were female. Their average educational level was one year of college. Their average age of first self-injury was 13.5 years, and the average number of acts was fifty. Only 18 percent felt that self-injury was no longer a problem for them.[11]

Famous People Who Have Self-Injured

It is possible that many people had not heard of self-injury until Princess Diana told the world, during a 1995 interview on British television, that she had cut her arms and legs while struggling with problems in her marriage. She told the person interviewing her, "You have so much pain inside yourself that you try and hurt yourself on the outside because you want help."[12]

She also told journalist Andrew Morton during an interview that she threw herself into a glass cabinet, slashed her wrists with a razor blade, and cut herself with a lemon slicer.[13]

Several other Hollywood stars have admitted to being self-injurers. Movie star Johnny Depp told *Details* magazine that he cut his arms to record strong emotions. Christina Ricci reported in *Rolling Stone* that she used bottle caps and a heated lighter on her arms. Angelina Jolie and Roseanne Barr

Princess Diana was one of the first famous people to admit to being a self-injurer.

have both said they injured themselves, but they did not give many details.[14]

The first question most people ask when they hear about people injuring themselves is "Why?" followed by "But doesn't it hurt?" We will look at the answers to those questions.

Is It Self-Injury or Extreme Body Modification?

Tattooing and body piercing have become very popular, and some people have taken them to a new level. People are piercing unusual body parts such as cheeks, lips, nipples and genitals. Some are covering their entire bodies with tattoos or making their tattoos three-dimensional by having Teflon placed under parts of the design. Others are using hot metal to brand scars into their skin.

Are these practices the same as self-injury? The answer is no, because they are done for different reasons.

People who decorate their bodies are doing it to express themselves or to make themselves more beautiful. People who self-injure are trying to cope with their emotions. They are trying to make themselves feel better by expressing their emotional pain through physical injury.

A second difference is in the area of control. People who decorate their bodies are in control of what they do. It is something they want to do. People who self-injure are often out of control. They are driven to hurt themselves even though they may not want to.[15]

Statistics About Self-Injurers

Dr. Armando R. Favazza and Karen Conterio gave a survey to 229 women who self-injured. They found some interesting things about them:

- 54 percent of the self-injurers said their childhoods were unhappy.
- 62 percent reported childhood abuse.
- 72 percent said they usually feel empty inside.
- 73 percent said they cannot find words to express their feelings.
- 75 percent said they are a burden to others.
- 67 percent said no one understands them.
- 82 percent said they want to stop the emotional pain.
- 69 percent said they are scared when they get close to someone.
- 21 percent said they have no friends, but 27 percent said they have many friends.
- 20 percent like the attention self-injury gets them.
- 35 percent said they do not know how to get positive attention.
- 75 percent used multiple methods to self-injure.
- 50 percent said they had self-injured more than fifty times.
- 25 percent liked to rub their scars and thought of them as a "badge of courage."
- 72 percent self-injured to control a racing mind, 65 percent to relax, 58 percent to feel less depressed, and 47 percent to feel less lonely.[16]

3

Why Do People Do This?

Why? Because I'm a bad person. I just suffer way too much to be a good person. I didn't do it for attention—that's what people think but it's not true.

Diane, age 24, active self-injurer[1]

It is very hard for most people to understand why someone would choose to injure his or her own body. Most people would so much prefer to avoid pain that they cannot imagine cutting or burning their own flesh.

Researchers have come up with a list of the major reasons why people self-injure:

- Relief from feelings and intense emotions
- A way of coping, to make themselves feel better
- A way to make themselves feel "real" or to feel something when they are emotionally numb
- To feel a rush of pleasure, like a "runner's high"

- To physically express emotional pain
- To communicate to others the extent of their pain
- To try to nurture themselves and heal their inner wounds
- To re-enact physical or sexual abuse
- To take control over something in their lives[2]

It was my secret little way of making myself feel better. I was afraid if I would stop that I would just blow up. I would just go crazy because I had no other way to deal with it. It felt like a release from pressure. I didn't think of it as pain, I thought of it as, "Oh, finally I can breathe" like coming up from under water.

Megan, age 22, former self-injurer[3]

A Learned Coping Method

"I think it happens when a person doesn't learn how to deal with emotions and feelings," says Dr. Laura Lees, a psychologist who works with teenagers and has had several self-injurers in her practice. "They don't learn other ways of coping so this becomes the main one they rely on. Usually it's the harder feelings to tolerate such as depression, anger, or rage that trigger it. The cutting gives them something visual to focus on, it distracts them from emotional distress they don't know how to deal with. Self-injurers are not 'crazy'—they are trying to find a way to cope with feelings or problems they have no other way to cope with."[4]

She says that recovering from a physical hurt is faster and easier than recovering from intense emotional pain. "Physical pain will end at some time," she says, "but if a person has an emotional problem that isn't being addressed, it just doesn't go away." She points out that, in general, people who self-injure are not trying to commit suicide. Their motivation is not to kill themselves, but to cope with life.[5]

> *It's just relief. I think I started doing it mainly because it was like punishing myself and was a relief from guilt.*
>
> Sarah, age 18, struggling self-injurer[6]

The Link With Abuse

One of the most frequent reasons why people self-injure is because they were physically or sexually abused as children. One research study involving 147 women who were self-injurers showed that their behavior was linked with sexual abuse, physical abuse, or both.[7]

In a different study, Dr. Favazza's pioneering research showed that 50 percent of self-injurers were sexually abused as children. According to him, sexual abuse can cause permanent damage to a child's emotional development.[8]

Some experts think abuse can actually do damage to a child's developing nervous system. Bessel van der Kolk, an associate professor of psychiatry at Harvard University and past president of the International Society of Traumatic Stress Studies, studied the effects of trauma on children. He found that severe trauma changes the structure and chemistry of the brain and parts of the nervous system that regulate stress. He says the child may become "hardwired" in a permanent state of fear and anxiety.[9]

> *Before every episode [of self-injury] I feel emotionally overwhelmed. The sight of my blood seems to release unbearable tension.*
>
> 39-year-old schoolteacher, active self-injurer[10]

Living With Chaos

"Another factor is being raised in a chaotic household where there are no limits, no boundaries, and the child never knows what the rules are," says Dr. Lees. "Such people internalize the constant confusion. They are always on edge and don't have any way to soothe themselves. They take all that 'craziness' and focus it into themselves and their bodies. They may think they are doing bad things to cause this constant confusion, so they cut themselves. They deal with that instead of telling Mom or Dad 'I'm really angry with you.'"[11]

She also points out that cutting is fast becoming the "in" thing to do among teenagers; some are doing it to be part of the group, not because they do not know how to cope in any other way. "It's a fad, it's what kids are doing now instead of getting into eating disorders," she says. "It's coming out the same way anorexia did during the 1980s."[12]

> *Most of all, the desire to injure myself comes when I feel like I have failed at something or when I feel as though someone close to me is going to leave me.*
>
> Anonymous female, age 32, active self-injurer[13]

Brain Chemicals

Some experts believe there is a brain chemistry problem that may underlie self-injury. Some researchers who measure the levels of chemicals in the brain have found a lower level of serotonin, a brain chemical that influences mood, in people who cut. Some patients have been helped by taking a drug that increases serotonin levels, such as Prozac, an antidepressant drug that affects brain chemistry.[14]

Some experts think the act of cutting or burning may produce increased levels of the brain chemicals that cause a person to feel good. A runner may experience the same feeling because of chemicals released in the brain during exercise; that is often called a "runner's high."[15] Some people have described cutting as an addiction to those chemicals. But Dr. Favazza says it is a habit, not a true addiction in which the body becomes physically dependent on a drug.[16]

The "high" some people receive from self injury is often compared to a "runner's high."

The chemical release may also be why many self-injurers say they do not feel any pain. Others, however, do say they feel pain, but that they need to feel it. "It's part of their motivation," says Dr. Lees. "It's easier to deal with that pain than it is to deal with their emotional pain. Having to deal with the wound and pain distracts them from their emotional distress. They have control over how deep, how long, how often they cut—but not the emotional pain."[17] Many self-injurers report that after the initial pain of the injury, they feel peaceful and calm, like their tension has been released.

Megan's Story

"I started burning myself when I was about fourteen. I had an aunt I was really close to who was an alcoholic. She died right in front of me, and I thought for a long time that it was my fault. But I didn't tell anyone that for a long time.

"I was playing with a lighter one day and I burned my finger accidentally. I was feeling the pain in my finger so much I didn't think about other stuff. I was like, 'Oh, this is cool.' My finger was all wrapped up and people were paying attention to me.

"After that I just kept doing it like once or twice a week and I hid it. I would only burn my arms and I always wore long sleeves.

"My mom and dad got divorced when I was little and my dad wasn't really a big part of my life. He was an alcoholic, too, and he made my mom's life miserable. He was pretty much a loser.

"My grandmother was the one who really raised me because my mother worked. She was really strict. She was very concerned about how I looked; I had to be skinny and walk and sit straight. A lot of the time I felt I couldn't live up to that, I couldn't handle the pressure. I couldn't handle not talking about my feelings. I couldn't handle trying to live up to my grandmother's expectations. I couldn't handle my mom never being there. So this was my secret little way of making myself feel better.

Megan's Story continued

"I never told anyone because I didn't want them to make me stop. I was afraid that if I stopped I would just blow up. I would go crazy because I couldn't find another way to deal with it. I started doing both burning and cutting; the cutting made more blood but the burning lasted longer. I stopped eating, too.

"I started going to therapy, but I didn't tell the therapist about the burning because I was afraid she would make me stop. When I was sixteen I tried to kill myself and the hospital set up therapy [with someone new]. She noticed my arms. She just started asking questions about it, she was never shocked, and she didn't act like what I was doing was wrong. She didn't try to make me stop right away. That's why I wasn't afraid to talk to her about it, that's what helped.

"We would make little deals like I'd only do it once a day, or I would snap a rubber band on my arm, or do something else that would help. And I went on some medication.

"Now I feel great. I still have really hard days but I don't feel like hurting myself. I shouldn't say never, but I haven't in, like, two years. I got married last year and we just had a baby, and things are going really well. Life is pretty much on the upswing."

Megan, age 22, former self-injurer[21]

Cutting myself . . . acts as an outlet for . . . internal pain, like it's all running out of me, like water out of a tap.

Anonymous female, age 17, active self-injurer[18]

Mental health experts who classify types of mental illness do not describe all self-injurers as mentally ill. However, the behavior is sometimes linked with mental disorders. That issue will be explored in the next chapter.

Injury gives me focus . . . I cannot seem to focus and stop the spinning or emotions/ideas and thoughts . . . Self-injury gives me a temporary peace.

Anonymous male, age 26, active self-injurer[19]

Some people who self-injure have rituals that can become as important to them as the cutting itself. They may choose only certain tools and certain places, or want special music in the background. Others have no such rituals.

"People usually have a preferred method of self-injury. But in the case of rituals, some do and some don't," says Dr. Laura Lees. "I've had patients who just hack away, and I've had others who are very deliberate in the kinds of cutting or burning and the way they do it."[20]

4

Mental Illnesses Linked With Self-Injury

While experts tell us that many people who self-injure are not mentally ill, some are. Self-injury is a factor in several different mental illness diagnoses.

Self-injury is in the *DSM-IV Diagnostic and Statistical Manual of Mental Disorders*, which is used by mental health professionals to diagnose mental illness. It lists the criteria for many different types of illness. The book does not list self-injury as a diagnosis by itself. Instead, it makes self-injury part of the criteria for several other diagnoses: borderline personality disorder (BPD), a movement disorder that is part of some types of mental retardation, and disorders in which a person fakes various illnesses.[1] In other words, self-injury may be a "symptom" of one of these other illnesses.

However, Dr. Favazza thinks self-injury can also be part of major depression and obsessive-compulsive disorder.[2] Other experts believe it could be part of eating disorders, post-traumatic stress disorder, and anxiety or panic disorder.[3]

Borderline Personality Disorder

I've been diagnosed with BPD—that's just one of them. I've also got problems with anxiety and manic depression. I'm on all kinds of medication, I'm not sure they help. I've been in a hospital day program but I'm not in that now. I'm just in a support group.

Diane, age 24, active self-injurer[4]

Borderline personality disorder (BPD) is a serious personality disorder that can cause patients and their families great pain. People with BPD seem to be frightened all the time that the people they love will leave them. In trying to stop that from happening, they behave in ways that end up causing conflict—so much so that they may actually wind up driving the person away. They often yell at people they love and may do violent things like starting fires or driving recklessly.

The *DSM-IV* lists nine traits linked with BPD: fear of abandonment, a pattern of unstable relationships, not having a good sense of self, being impulsive, injuring oneself, having intense mood swings, having chronic feelings of being "empty," showing intense flashes of anger, and having periods of feeling removed from reality. To be diagnosed with BPD, a person must show five of these traits.[5] Many people who do not have BPD show some of these traits, but it is the number and the severity of the traits that point to BPD.

Although self-injury is one of the traits used to diagnose BPD, not all people who self-injure have it. One study showed that only 48 percent of the self-injurers in that study met the criteria for BPD.[6]

Eating Disorders

I developed an eating disorder. I'm 5'6" and I probably got down to about 108 pounds. I would wear my heaviest clothes when I'd go to therapy so when I got weighed it wouldn't seem like I'd lost weight. Nobody knew then that I was also hurting myself but I still thought they would make me stop.

Megan, age 22, former self-injurer[7]

The most common eating disorders are anorexia and bulimia. Anorexics eat so little they literally starve themselves. Bulimics eat, but then force themselves to throw up or otherwise purge the food. In either case, their

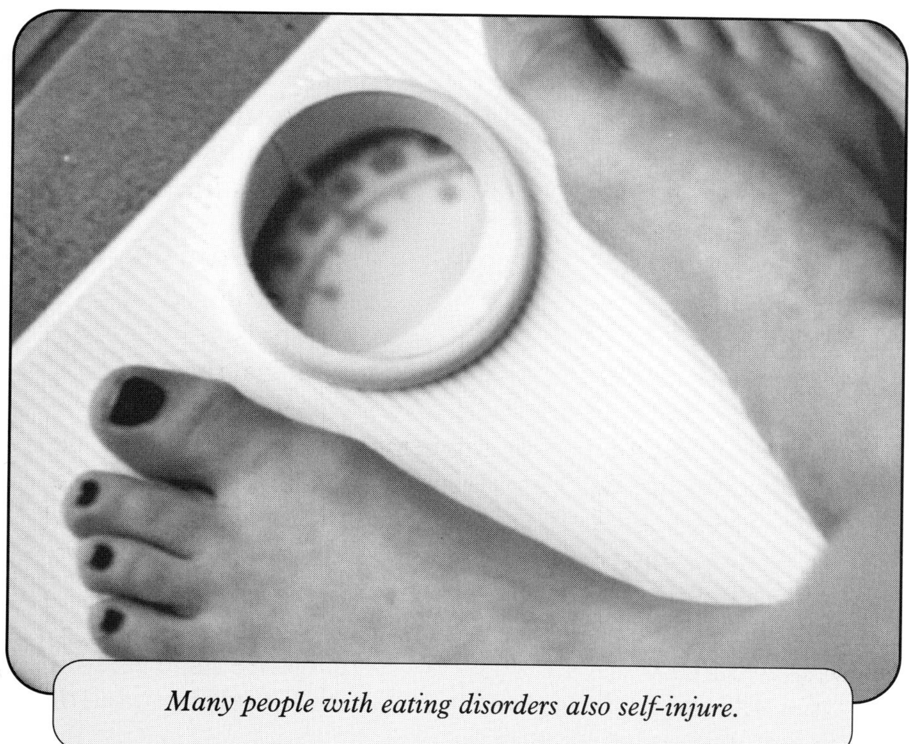

Many people with eating disorders also self-injure.

goal is to control their bodies and become as thin as possible. People with these disorders do not see themselves as thin, however. No matter how bone thin they become, they still think of themselves as fat.

Self-injury occurs with many eating disorder patients. One study by Dr. Favazza showed that of 495 outpatients being treated for an eating disorder, 26 percent self-injured.[8] In a different study done with his associate, Karen Conterio, half of the self-injurers either were or had been anorexic or bulimic.[9] They also found that, among eating disorder patients, self-injury was the hardest behavior for them to give up.[10]

"I think you see self-injury in the population of eating disorder patients who are the sickest," says Dr. Lees. "Does the eating disorder or the self-injury come first? That's a flip of the coin. Patients will often force themselves to purge and purge until they're puking blood. That's a method of self-injury, a way to hurt themselves because they don't know what to do with all the hurt inside."[11]

Major Depression, Bipolar Disorder, and Other Diagnoses

> *I get depressed, I don't know why. If anything goes wrong, at school or at home, if I forget my homework and a teacher shouts at me . . . silly stuff, really. But after I self-injure I feel disgusted at myself, I feel as if, no matter how hard I try, I can't do anything right.*
>
> Anonymous female, age 15, active self-injurer[12]

Major depression is not the same as "having the blues." Major depression is an illness that affects the whole person. Mental health professionals use a list of symptoms to suggest major depression: mood disturbance, not enjoying life, change in eating patterns, change in sleeping patterns, not thinking clearly, change in concentration, change in physical activity, loss of energy, and thinking about, or trying, suicide.[13]

Bipolar disorder, which used to be called manic-depressive disorder, is similar to major depression in that the person has deep lows of depression. But then they swing to highs when they are filled with energy. They may go for days without sleep, and feel they can accomplish almost anything.[14]

Self-injury is sometimes seen in these patients. Since an underlying cause of depression and bipolar disorder is linked with the brain chemical serotonin, it is possible that this chemical may be linked to self-injury also.[15]

There are two other diagnoses in which self-injury may play a minor part. One is obsessive-compulsive disorder, in which people feel they must go through many rituals. Hair-pulling is sometimes part of the illness.[16] The other is post-traumatic stress disorder, which can happen when a person has experienced an extremely traumatic event. Patients can have many symptoms, including nightmares and flashbacks, and sometimes they self-injure.[17]

Many people who self-injure do not have any of these mental illnesses. All of them, however, are taking a great risk. We will look next at the dangers of self-injury.

5

Dangers in Self-Injury

People who self-injure are taking some very big risks. They may think that a shallow slice with a razor on the skin of their arm or leg is no big deal, and many times it is not. But there are other times when they may cut just a little too deep and do themselves real harm. Or they could not realize that the tool they are using is dirty and introduce germs into their bodies. And, however they self-injure, they will probably be left with scars.

When Self-Injury Goes Too Far

"The most common thing I see in the emergency room [with self-injurers] is infection," says Marlene Melzer-Lang, M.D., an emergency room doctor at Children's Hospital, part of the Medical College of Wisconsin. "Even if they wipe themselves with alcohol, they can get infections in their skin which may need antibiotics. In unusual cases they

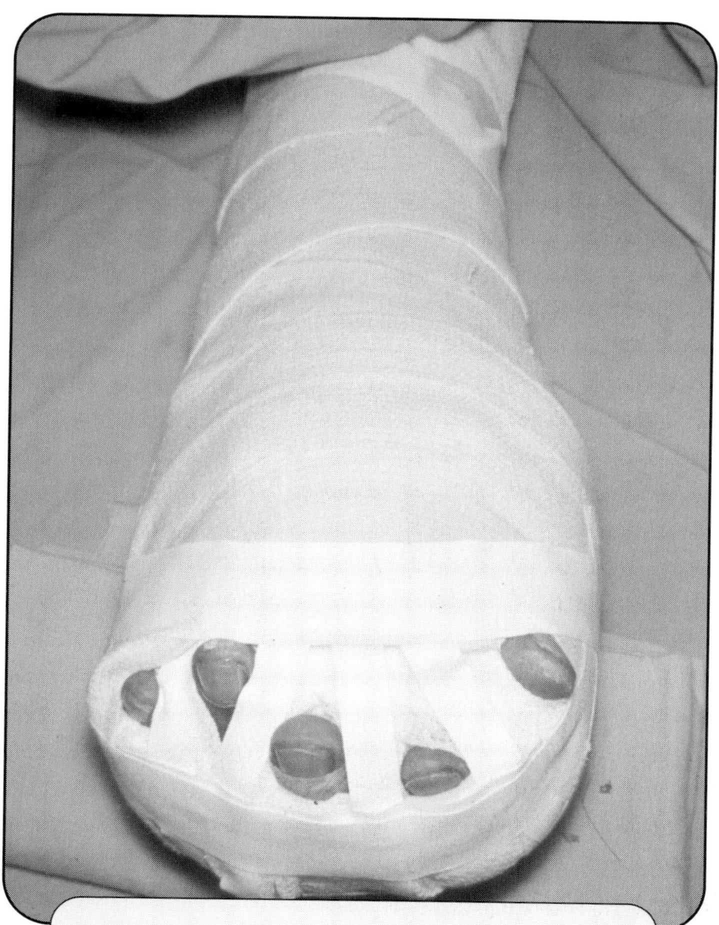

Self-injurers can cut too deeply and sever tendons which control hand motions. Surgery may be needed to restore function.

could even need an antibiotic put directly into the vein, which would mean staying in the hospital."[1]

She points out that it would take a very deep slice on the arm to cut the tendons that lie underneath the skin, but it could happen. "The tendons in the inner arm are what make you bend your fingers. You could lose function in your fingers."[2]

She has also seen someone sever the artery doctors use to count the pulse. "That one needed surgery to repair," she says. "You could bleed to death from that cut but it would be a slow and painful death. It would take many hours."[3]

Cutting on the thigh is less likely to cause severe bleeding or to cut muscle or tendon because there is at least an inch of fat even on a thin person's thigh, she says. However, that does not mean cutting on the thigh is safe. "If you went deeper than that fat, you would cut muscle—the quadriceps, the big thigh muscle. It's quite thick, two to three inches, so it would be hard to slice through the whole thing. The arteries there are very deep."[4]

But, she says, the arteries and veins in the groin are closer to the surface. "You could bleed to death from a cut there," she says.[5]

Cutting on the chest, especially on the breasts, is less likely to produce bleeding. "The breast is mostly fat and gland tissue," she says. "But I know of a case where a woman self-injured her breast, hid it from people, got a bad infection in her bloodstream and nearly died from it."[6] The possible complications of infection include fever, shock, and even death if it is not treated, she says.

Scarring

Some people who self-injure do not want to hide their scars. "People who self-injure will view scars with a degree of pride—they are like battle scars, a badge of honor, proof of what they have endured," says Marilee Strong.[7]

"[They say] I survived the battle, no one is going to hurt me as much as I hurt myself," adds Karen Conterio, founder of the S.A.F.E. treatment program for self-injurers, located in Berwyn, Illinois.[8]

But not everyone feels that way. Some self-injurers cover their scars with long pants and sleeves even in the hottest weather. Others think they can have the scars removed, that it is not a big deal to have them taken off with plastic surgery.

Unfortunately, they are wrong, says George Korkos, M.D., a plastic surgeon who has a lot of experience in scar removal.

"Anytime you cut the surface of the skin you'll have a permanent scar. Any way you look at it, it's permanent. Forever. You can underline that—forever," he says.[9]

Different types of cuts leave different types of scars, and they all present different challenges, he says.

"Razors and very sharp knives make a very fine scar. Sometimes they are parallel, like a ladder," he says. "It's very difficult to improve them because there isn't enough skin to close in a fine fashion. There may be just a half inch between the scars and you just can't fix them. It's very hard to get a good result."[10]

On the other hand, deep or jagged cuts may make thick, lumpy scars. "That kind of scar shows up much more at talking distance," he says. "They are difficult scars to improve. Again, there isn't a lot of skin to work with, and it is not loose enough to bring it together. It is possible to cut thick scars out, trim the layers and close them in a finer fashion, but there still will be a scar. Sometimes a laser can take off one layer of skin at a time and make them look a little better. Skin grafts are not a possibility. They would look like a patch and show more than the scar."[11]

Burns, especially cigarette burns, can be almost impossible to remove, he says. "Cigarette burns are what is called ultra-pigmented, a little circle of darker color. If you do that many times in a large area there is nothing that can be done about it. Sometimes a chemical peel will help a little bit, but usually I just throw up my hands," he says. "Sometimes there's a limit to what plastic surgery can do."[12]

Infection, he says, makes scars worse. "They become wider, very hard and irregular especially if there is constant picking at the scar. During the healing process the body produces cells called fibroblasts to promote healing. Sometimes you get overproduction and you will see very ropey scars."[13]

He points out that the darker the person's skin tone, the more the person may scar. Black skin often forms scars that are thicker and heavier than those in white skin. They can be impossible to remove.

Plastic surgery to remove scars does not come cheap. "Fees vary, but you are talking thousands of dollars," he says. "You need an operating room, a doctor, an anesthesiologist—a lot of money and you could still end up with scars."[14]

It is better to get help for the problems causing self-injury rather than wait until scars, both physical and psychological, are severe. We will look next at ways to treat people who self-injure.

6

Treating People Who Self-Injure

[My therapist] has helped me more than I can say, but you have to trust the person. You have to be able to tell them anything and know that your secret is safe with them. I know that my secret was always safe with her. She just helped me to stop one day at a time.

Megan, age 22, former self-injurer[1]

"Self-injury is definitely treatable," says Dr. Laura Lees. "But treatment is long term. You can work on teaching people what their feelings are, how to identify them and then what alternate methods of coping they can use. That can certainly replace their self-injury. People have to learn how to tolerate their feelings without responding in an impulsive way and that takes time. But people can stop."[2]

The fact that Parker, Megan, and many others have stopped injuring themselves shows that Dr. Lees is right.

People can stop. There are a number of different ways to help them do that.

Being Ready

Because stopping self-injury can be very hard, the person has to be ready and want to do it. A Web site that offers advice and support to self-injurers says a person should have several things in place in order to stop. Remember, this is not professional advice but thoughts from people who have coped with self-injury.

- A support system of friends, family, and professional help
- Two people to call when the impulse to injure comes
- A list of ten things to do instead of self-injuring
- A place to go to get away from where the self-injury usually happens
- Being able to get rid of razors, scissors, or other things used to self-injure
- Telling at least two people about trying to stop
- Being willing to feel a little uncomfortable and scared sometimes[3]

Experts say that some people can stop self-injuring on their own. As some people get older, issues that troubled them as teens may fade away; they no longer feel they need cutting as a way of coping. Or they may learn what issues drive their self-injury and be able to resolve them.

But most people need professional help. Marilee Strong says, "Peeling away the complex web of coping mechanisms they have used to survive and healing the deeper internal

Sometimes professional help is necessary to overcome self-injury.

wounds is a painstaking process that requires an extraordinary commitment on the part of the patient."[4]

There is no one way that works with all people since people self-injure for so many different reasons. Generally there are three parts to treatment: medication to help get the impulse under control, behavior modification or learning new coping skills to help stop cutting, and exploring the deeper issues causing the behavior.

Medication

"Almost every time somebody is injuring themselves repeatedly, there is a disturbance of the chemical functioning in the brain cells," says Richard Gerhardstein, M.D., a psychiatrist who works with self-injurers.[5]

The first drug most doctors try is an antidepressant. "We don't usually use the older antidepressants because they don't work as well and an overdose can kill," he says. "The newer drugs such as Prozac, Zoloft, or Paxil for example, work well and are much less dangerous."[6]

He says an antidepressant used for obsessive-compulsive behavior, Luvox, can be useful in some cases of self-injury. If the person has wild mood swings, a drug called lithium, a mood stabilizer used for bipolar disorder, can help. In rare cases, an anti-psychotic drug could be used. "The newer ones such as Risperdal are good because they are weaker than the older drugs and you can tailor the dose better," he says.[7]

"There is a lot of trial and error in finding the right drug," he points out. "One drug won't work for everybody. Sometimes they don't work at all. Sometimes they work for a while and then stop working. And, the medication only treats the symptoms—you still have to get at the underlying issues through psychotherapy."[8]

Every drug has side effects, Dr. Gerhardstein warns. Sometimes they make the person sleepy; sometimes they have the opposite effect leading to a shaky, nervous feeling. They can also cause stomach upset.[9]

The drugs are not addictive. "If you stop taking some of them too fast you may get a reaction, become jumpy and anxious, but that's not a true addiction. You have to taper them down very slowly," he says. "These drugs do not cause a person to feel high so there is no illegal street market for them."[10]

Learning New Ways to Cope

"The hard part of treatment is that no other coping mechanisms have the 'quick fix,' the immediate numbing or blocking emotional distress that the self-harm does," says Dr. Lees. "Patients have to learn alternate methods—and that could be anything. When the desire to self-harm comes, it could be just stopping, sitting, and breathing. It could be calling a friend, writing in a journal, going for a walk, taking a shower, petting the dog. It could be getting away from the objects used to self-injure. The basic thing is to break the cycle of immediately going to the self-injuring behavior."[11]

According to Kristin Niekerk, a psychotherapist who works with eating disorder and self-injury patients, it is important that the therapist not react negatively when a patient first reveals that he or she is self-injuring. "The therapist should never say something like, 'Oh, that's gross, you have to stop it!'" she says. "He or she should first find out some facts. How long has it been going on? What

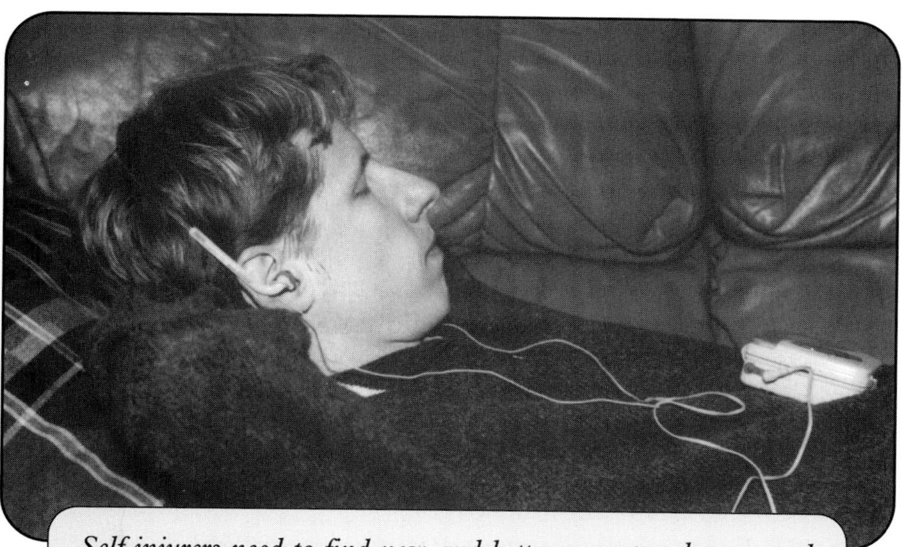

Self-injurers need to find new and better ways to relax, control stress, and have fun.

happened the first time to set it off? The therapist needs to remain calm and low key because sometimes people who cut have a personality disorder and to make a big deal out of it may feed into their problems."[12]

The next step would be getting a better understanding of why the person is self-injuring. Many times he or she may not be sure. "We look at the situations that make the person want to cut, or feel like he or she can't handle things any other way," Niekerk says. "From there we work on learning new coping skills. The person needs something that can break into the cycle of being upset, not knowing how to deal with it, and numbing out by cutting."[13]

She guides the patient into creating his or her own list of alternate things to do. "I look for a list of at least twenty different things," she says. "Sometimes the therapist will first work on getting the person to just delay the cutting for a time because stopping right away may not be realistic. Sometimes the therapist will write a contract with the person. It will be very specific and have real consequences for breaking it."[14]

Some therapists, she says, may use a technique called "extinction." For a session or two, the therapist and patient talk about nothing but the cutting until the person is so tired of talking about it that he or she may stop doing it. This technique works best with patients who have a personality disorder; it does not work for everyone.[15]

As underlying issues are uncovered, the therapist will help the patient learn ways to deal with each one. For example, she says, if a teenager says she cuts because she cannot deal with her parents, the therapist will help her work on communication skills.[16]

She also points out that what happens between therapist and patient is confidential. "At the first session I always tell patients that there are only three times when

I could legally break confidentiality: if they are at risk for seriously harming themselves, at risk for hurting others, or if someone is hurting them," she says. "Otherwise, what is said is strictly between us. If someone tells me she is cutting, I will work with her to be able to talk to her parents about it. I won't go to the parents and say, 'Did you know your child is cutting?'"[17]

Dealing With What Is Underneath

We learned to record our feelings in books called impulse logs. We would write down an impulse (like wanting to injure yourself), the feelings behind it (sadness or anger), and what would happen if we followed the impulse (like feeling worse or wanting to injure yourself more). Before, I had trouble identifying my feelings. But the writing really helped.

Anonymous female, recovered self-injurer,
telling her story in a magazine[18]

While teaching new coping skills is an important part of treatment, by itself it may not be enough, especially if the person has abuse or other trauma in his or her background. Those issues need to be dealt with also.

"You have to identify why this is happening, what causes the emotional stress that drives the behavior," says Dr. Lees. "You need to do the emotional work while helping them with behavior. Putting those two things together can be very effective."[19]

Getting at the underlying issues, especially if they include abuse, can be painful, hard work and it can take a long time. The patient must have a trusting relationship with the therapist in order to feel comfortable looking at things which may have hurt deeply. "All of the trauma and crises that spawned the cutting will be played out in the doctor-patient relationship," says Marilee Strong.[20]

Different therapists will use different techniques to work with patients on the emotional issues. Talking out the issues will take a lot of the time. Some other methods could include:

- **Keeping a journal**—Sometimes writing down feelings, especially ones which trigger self-injury, can help.
- **Ego strengthening**—In this approach, the therapist tries to find positive things about the patient to raise self-esteem.
- **Guided imagery**—The therapist helps the patient see a peaceful, relaxing place in his or her mind, a place to go to when stress becomes unbearable. The patient may also visualize stopping the self-injury, doing something positive instead.
- **"Re-thinking" techniques**—These methods go under different names such as behavioral reframing or cognitive-behavioral treatment, but they all work on teaching the person to think differently. For example, if a person thinks of herself as shy and unable to talk to people, the therapist may help her to see herself as more friendly and outgoing, and help her learn some conversational skills. As the person changes the way he or she thinks, behavior can also change.

- **Reinforcing the positive**—In this technique, the therapist praises any positive change, no matter how tiny, and gives little attention to "bad" behavior.[21]

Getting treatment is very important, says Dr. Lees. "People need to stop this behavior because it will never solve their problems," she says. "Even if the person gets short-term relief by cutting, that doesn't create long-term relief. It doesn't take away the pain. Pain always comes back and you have to self-injure more. That just creates another problem and makes the original problem harder to address."[22]

I don't think that I'll ever consider myself stopped because I could do it tomorrow or in ten years. It doesn't seem like stopping to me. But right now I haven't done it for ten or eleven weeks and that's a lot better than last year.

Sarah, age 19, recently stopped self-injury[23]

The S.A.F.E. Program

The S.A.F.E. (Self Abuse Finally Ends) Alternatives Program is an inpatient hospital program started by Karen Conterio and Dr. Wendy Lader in 1985. The program is for self-injurers aged twelve and above. It includes a thirty-day hospital treatment program and outpatient care. Patients participate in education, support groups, group and individual therapy, and aftercare. Patients must sign a safety contract for the time they are in the program, find five new ways to handle impulses, participate in all groups, and complete fifteen writing assignments about their issues.[24]

7

When a Friend Self-Injures

The temperature outside is 90 degrees with humidity to match; why does my friend go to the beach wearing jeans and a long-sleeved shirt?

Prom dress shopping is fun—but why does my friend want to go into the fitting room alone and only try on dresses with lacy sleeves?

A spot of blood oozes through my friend's sleeve. "Oh, it's just an accident, the knife slipped when I was peeling an apple," she says. Do those kinds of "accidents" happen often?

It is possible that your friend is a self-injurer. She may be hiding scars by never letting her arms or legs show. She may have endless excuses about breaking a glass, dropping a hot curling iron, or cutting herself while shaving. Other clues include not being able to handle emotions very well, being isolated and having few friends, and not wanting to undress in gym class or on sports teams in front of others.

When people learn that someone they care about is self-injuring, the most common reactions are shock, anger, frustration, and guilt. A friend of a self-injurer needs to understand those feelings so he or she can move past them.

A big part of shock is denial. It is often easier to ignore the clues, pretend not to see the scars, and avoid talking about it. But that is not helpful to the friend. "People who injure themselves are in a great deal of psychological distress. To deny this distress will communicate that you are not interested . . . It is important you do not deny the reality . . . of the situation," says psychologist Tracy Alderman.[1] Alderman was writing to mental health professionals about how to help self-injurers, but her advice is also helpful for friends of self-injurers.

Self-injurers often wear long sleeves and pants, even in the hottest weather, to hide their scars.

Another common response is anger. People may be angry because their friend lied to them for a long time about self-injuring. They may be angry and frustrated because they cannot stop the friend, and just saying "Don't do that anymore" will not help.[2]

Friends may also feel guilty, wondering "Why didn't I see this sooner?" or "Did I do something to make my friend do this?" The answers are that you probably did not see it because your friend was very good at hiding it. And chances are that you had nothing to do with the reasons why he or she did it.

Another thought that many teenagers have when they find out a friend self-injures is, "I can fix this; I can help them to get over it." That is a natural thing to feel. No one likes to see someone in pain. We all want to do something to end it. "However," says Alderman, "without the proper education and training, helping could do more damage than good."[3]

Here are some things a teen should and should not do if he or she finds out that a friend is self-injuring:

- Do not be afraid to talk about it. Ignoring the scars just feeds into the person's need to hide what he or she is doing. "Ignoring something does not make it disappear," says Alderman. "Silence makes a very powerful statement."[4]
- On the other hand, do not overreact. "If you notice someone is self-injuring, certainly ask them about it but don't make a big deal about their injuries," says Dr. Lees. "Some of them are very proud of what they have done and would like everyone to see; you don't want to give that kind of attention to someone who self-injures."[5]

- Be aware that asking about self-injuring can be a trigger for the person to self-injure even more. "Because you never know what is going to set off self-injury, the best thing is to tell an adult," says Dr. Lees.[6]
- If the person does not want to talk about it, do not force the issue. Remind them that you are there and always willing to listen.[7]
- Let the person know that he or she does not have to self-injure to get your attention, or your caring. Make it clear that you love and care about the person and self-injury will not change that.[8]
- Set limits on what you can and cannot do. It is okay to tell the friend that you will not talk while they are in the act of self-injuring—that is a reasonable limit. Saying "I will not be your friend if you ever do that again" is not okay because the threat of losing your friendship may make the problem worse.[9]
- Offer a safe place or something else to do when the urge to injure comes. Taking someone out for ice cream, a movie, or just a walk when they are upset can be helpful. Saying, "You can sleep over at my house when you are trying not to hurt yourself," might be helpful.[10]
- Trying to force someone to change will not work. Telling someone you will never speak to them again if the self-injury continues will just make them go back to keeping it a secret. A "guilt trip" will not work either. Saying,

Friends can help distract a person when they are making an effort not to self-injure.

"How could you do that and gross out all your friends?" will not make someone stop. It may make things worse.[11]

- Never help the person keep self-injury a secret. A self-injurer may ask you not to tell and may become angry if you do. "It is better that your friend hate you or is angry at you than that you continue to let her hurt herself," says Dr. Lees. "This should never be kept secret because it will only get worse over time. Your friend may be mad, but that's better than her continuing to hurt herself."[12]

- Last, and most important, do not try to be the only one helping the person. Realize that this problem is far beyond the ability of a teenager to manage. You must get help. You must tell an adult who will be able to get the person to professional help. Tell your parents, tell a teacher or guidance counselor at school, tell a minister, rabbi, priest, or cleric. That can be very hard to do, and your friend may be angry. But a teenage friend cannot take the place of a mental health professional. That is asking way too much of yourself, and in the long run, it will not help the friend.[13]

Chapter Notes

Chapter 1. Parker's Story

1. Personal interview with "Parker," May 11, 2001.

Chapter 2. What Is This Thing Called Self-Injury?

1. Telephone interview with Diane, February 12, 2001.

2. Deb Martinson, "Self-Injury: A Quick Guide to the Basics," 1996, <www.palace.net/~llama/psych/guide.html> (January 26, 2001).

3. Deb Martinson, "What Self-Injury Is," 1996, <www.palace.net/~llama/psych/fwhat.html> (January 26, 2001).

4. Ibid.

5. Deb Martinson, "Who Self-Injures?" 1996, <www.palace.net/~llama/psych/who.html> (January 26, 2001); Armando R. Favazza and Karen Conterio, "Plight of Chronic Self-Mutilators," *Community Mental Health Journal*, vol. 24, no. 1, Spring 1988, p. 25.

6. *Secret Cutting*, Lifetime original movie, copyright 2000 by Longbow Productions, LLC, Lancaster Gate Entertainment, Carlton America.

7. Deb Martinson, "Who Self-Injures?"

8. Marilee Strong, quoted in personal interview on Lifetime Television, *Hidden Addictions: Celebrity Stories*, copyright 2000, USA Cable Entertainment, LLC and shown following *Secret Cutting*.

9. Marilee Strong, *A Bright Red Scream: Self-Mutilation and the Language of Pain* (New York: Penguin Putnam Inc., 1998), p. 25.

10. Karen Suyemoto, Ph.D. and Xochitl Kountz, M.S., "Self Mutilation," *The Prevention Researcher*, vol. 7, no. 4, November 2000, p. 2.

11. Favazza and Conterio, p. 25.

12. Strong, p. 19.

13. Ibid., p. 19.

14. Lifetime Television, *Hidden Addictions: Celebrity Stories*, copyright 2000, USA Cable Entertainment, LLC.

15. Personal interview with Laura Lees, Psy. D., April 11, 2001, and Gina Ng, quoted in Tracy Alderman, Ph.D., "Helping Those Who Hurt Themselves," *The Prevention Researcher*, November 2000, vol. 7, no. 4, p. 5.

16. Armando Favazza and Karen Conterio, "Female Habitual Self-Mutilators," *Suicide Behavior in Mental Hospitals*, September 18, 1988.

Chapter 3. Why Do People Do This?

1. Telephone interview with Diane, February 12, 2001.

2. "Why Do People Engage in Self-Inflicted Violence?" *The Prevention Researcher*, November 2000, vol. 7, no. 4, p. 11; n.d., <http://www.family.institute.net/self-injury.htm>.

3. Telephone interview with Megan, March 5, 2001.

4. Personal interview with Laura Lees, Psy.D., April 13, 2001.

5. Ibid.

6. Telephone interview with Sarah, May 6, 2001.

7. Michael W. Widerman, et. al., "Bodily Self-Harm and Its Relationship to Childhood Abuse Among Women in a Primary Care Setting," *Violence Against Women*, February 1999, vol. 5, issue 2, p. 155.

8. Marilee Strong, *A Bright Red Scream: Self-Mutilation and the Language of Pain* (New York: Penguin Putnam Inc., 1998), p. 64.

9. Ibid., pp. 88–89.

10. Anonymous in Armando R. Favazza and Karen Conterio, "Plight of Chronic Self-Mutilators," *Community Mental Health Journal*, vol. 24, no. 1, Spring 1988, p. 26.

11. Personal interview with Laura Lees.

12. Ibid.

13. "Why do you self-injure," Internet postings page, quotes added January 19, 2001, 1998, <www.palace.net/~llama/psych/qwhy.html> (January 26, 2001).

14. Strong, p. 108.

15. Ibid., p. 106.

16. Ibid., p. 58.

17. Personal interview with Laura Lees.

18. "Why do you self-injure."

19. Ibid.

20. Personal interview with Laura Lees, and "Do You Have Rituals for SI?" 1998, <www.palace.net/~llama/psych/qrit.html> (January 26, 2000).

21. Telephone interview with Megan, March 5, 2001.

Chapter 4. Mental Illnesses Linked With Self-Injury

1. *Diagnostic and Statistical Manual of Mental Disorders*, 4th ed., (Washington, D.C.: American Psychiatric Association, 1994), p. 654; Additional background information from "Diagnoses Associated with Self-Injury," 1998, <www.palace.net/~llama/psych/ diag.html> (January 26, 2001).

2. Armando Favazza, "Why Patients Mutilate Themselves," *Hospital and Community Psychiatry*, February 1989, vol. 40, no. 2, p. 137.

3. "Diagnoses Associated with Self-Injury."

4. Telephone interview with Diane, February 12, 2001.

5. *Diagnostic and Statistical Manual of Mental Disorders*, p. 654.

6. "Diagnoses Associated with Self-Injury."

7. Telephone interview with Megan, March 5, 2001.

8. Armando Favazza, "Impulsive and Compulsive Self-Injurious Behavior in Bulimia Nervosa: Prevalence and Psychological Correlates," *The Journal of Nervous and Mental Disease*, quoted in *The Prevention Researcher*, November 2000, vol. 7, no. 4, pp. 8–10.

9. Marilee Strong, *A Bright Red Scream: Self-Mutilation and the Language of Pain* (New York: Penguin Putnam Inc., 1998), p. 116.

10. Ibid., p. 118.

11. Personal interview with Laura Lees, Psy.D., April 13, 2001.

12. "Why do you self-injure," Internet postings page, quotes added January 19, 2001, 1998, <www.palace.net/~llama/psych/qwhy.html> (January 26, 2001).

13. *Diagnostic and Statistical Manual of Mental Disorders*, p. 327.

14. Ibid., pp. 355–358; 362–363.

15. "Diagnoses Associated with Self-Injury."

16. *Diagnostic and Statistical Manual of Mental Disorders*, pp. 422–423; 672–673.

17. Ibid., pp. 427–429.

Chapter 5. Dangers in Self-Injury

1. Telephone Interview with Marlene Melser-Lang, M.D., May 14, 2001.
2. Ibid.
3. Ibid.
4. Ibid.
5. Ibid.
6. Ibid.
7. Lifetime Television, *Hidden Addictions: Celebrity Stories*, copyright 2000, USA Cable Entertainment, LLC.
8. Ibid.
9. Personal interview with George Korkos, M.D., April 30, 2001.
10. Ibid.
11. Ibid.
12. Ibid.
13. Ibid.
14. Ibid.

Chapter 6. Treating People Who Self-Injure

1. Telephone interview with Megan, March 5, 2001.
2. Personal interview with Laura Lees, Psy.D., April 13, 2001.
3. Adapted from a list found at, 1998, <www.palace.net/~llama/psych/self.html> (January 26, 2001).
4. Marilee Strong, *A Bright Red Scream: Self-Mutilation and the Language of Pain* (New York: Penguin Putnam Inc., 1998), p. 161.
5. Telephone interview with Dr. Richard Gerhardstein, April 30, 2001.
6. Ibid.
7. Ibid.
8. Ibid.
9. Ibid.
10. Ibid.
11. Personal interview with Laura Lees, Psy.D.
12. Personal interview with Kristin Niekerk, M.S., July 2, 2001.
13. Ibid.
14. Ibid.

15. Ibid.
16. Ibid.
17. Ibid.
18. Christine Roberts, "My Problem and How I Solved It: I Couldn't Stop Hurting Myself," *Good Housekeeping*, September 1999, vol. 229, issue 3, p. 104.
19. Personal interview with Laura Lees, Psy.D., April 13, 2001.
20. Strong, p. 165.
21. Moshe S. Torem, "A Practical Approach in the Treatment of Self-Inflicted Violence," *Journal of Holistic Nursing*, March 1995, vol. 13, issue 1, p. 37.
22. Personal interview with Laura Lees, Psy.D., April 13, 2001.
23. Telephone interview with Sarah, May 6, 2001.
24. S.A.F.E. Alternatives brochure: "A Comprehensive Treatment Program for Those Who Self-Injure," received April 2001.

Chapter 7. When a Friend Self-Injures

1. Tracy Alderman, Ph.D., "Helping Those Who Hurt Themselves," *The Prevention Researcher*, November 2000, vol. 7, no. 4, p. 5.
2. Ibid., p. 6.
3. Ibid.
4. Ibid.
5. Personal interview with Laura Lees, Psy.D., April 13, 2001.
6. Ibid.
7. "Help for Family and Friends," 1998, <www.palace.net/~llama/psych/ffriend.html> (January 26, 2001).
8. Ibid.
9. Ibid.
10. Ibid.
11. Ibid.
12. Personal interview with Laura Lees, Psy.D.
13. Ibid.

Glossary

alcohol—Isopropyl or rubbing alcohol is a disinfectant. Self-injurers often use it to keep their cuts or burns from becoming infected.

anorexia—An eating disorder in which people starve themselves.

antidepressants—Medications that correct chemical imbalances in the brain related to depression. People who self-injure are sometimes helped by taking antidepressants.

artery—A blood vessel that carries blood from the heart out to the body. Cutting an artery can result in bleeding to death.

bipolar disorder—A mental illness in which a person alternates between feeling very "high" and very depressed. Some people with bipolar disorder self-injure.

borderline personality disorder (BPD)—A personality disorder in which a person has many fears, including the fear that the people they love will leave them. They often behave violently; people with BPD often self-injure.

bulimia—An eating disorder in which people eat and then throw up.

coping skills—The things people do to handle stress. People who self-injure often do not have very good coping skills.

eating disorders—A condition in which people try to control their lives through controlling their weight. They may eat too little and become very thin, or overeat and become very heavy. Some people with eating disorders self-injure.

infection—When harmful bacteria gets into the body through a cut or some other means. Infection may cause a cut to become red, swollen and painful. Infections can cause serious injury or even death if they are not treated with antibiotics.

major depression—A condition, often caused by a chemical imbalance in the brain, in which a person becomes very sad and hopeless. True depression lasts a long time; it does not go away after a depressing event is over.

mental illness—Any of a wide variety of conditions in which a person's mind and emotions are considered abnormal. Mental illness is diagnosed by a licensed medical professional.

obsessive-compulsive disorder (OCD)—A mental illness in which a person cannot control his or her need to perform various rituals over and over again. Some people with this disorder self-injure.

post-traumatic stress disorder (PTSD)—A condition in which a person who has been through a terrible event has trouble getting beyond it and may mentally re-live it over and over. Some people with PTSD may self-injure.

psychiatrist—A medical doctor who has additional training in understanding the human mind and emotions. A psychiatrist helps people to understand and deal with their emotions and can prescribe medication.

psychologist—A mental health professional who helps people to understand their feelings and find ways to deal with them. A psychologist cannot prescribe medicine.

scars—Thick, raised tissue at the site of a cut or burn. People who self-injure usually have scars.

self-injury—The act of doing harm to one's own body, doing it alone, and doing something serious enough to damage tissue and, often, leave a scar. It can involve cutting, burning, or other methods.

serotonin—A brain chemical that helps keep people calm and feeling good. Researchers think people who self-injure may have low levels of serotonin.

sexual abuse—When someone has sexual contact with a child or with a person who cannot or does not give consent.

suicide—The act of taking one's own life. People who self-injure are usually not trying to commit suicide.

tendons—Structures in the body that connect bones. A tendon could be cut if someone cuts too deeply while self-injuring.

Further Reading

Clark, Alicia, M.A. *Coping with Self-Mutilation: A Helping Book for Teens Who Hurt Themselves*. New York: Rosen Group Publishing, 1999.

Kettlewell, Caroline. *Skin Game*. New York: Griffin Trade Paperback, 2000.

Lee, Jordan. *Coping With Self-Mutilation*. Minneapolis: Hazelden Information Education, 1999.

Strong, Marilee. *A Bright Red Scream: Self-Mutilation and the Language of Pain*. New York: Penguin Putnam Inc., 1998.

Turner, V.J. *Secret Scars: Uncovering and Understanding the Addiction of Self-Injury*. Minn.: Hazelden Information Education, 2002.

Internet Addresses

Note: Experts say that people who self-injure can be triggered by visiting Web sites or chat rooms that discuss self-injury.

HealthyPlace Self-Injury Community
<www.healthyplace.com/Communities/Self_Injury/site/>

Self-Injury: You are Not the Only One
<www.palace.net/~llama/psych/injury.html>

For More Information

S.A.F.E. Alternatives

MacNeal Hospital
1099 Gast Road
Bridgeman, MI 49106
1–800–DONTCUT (1–800–366–8288)
<www.safe-alternatives.com/>

The Cutting Edge (newsletter about self-injury)
P.O. Box 20819
Cleveland, OH 44120

Index